# Birth and Early Years of Gandhiji's Life

Mahatma Gandhi is one of the most revered names in Indian history. He was the political and ideological leader of India, also honoured as Father of our nation, he became an international symbol of the free India. He played a very important role in the Indian freedom movement. He is lovingly called as Bapu. His teachings of 'Ahinsa' and 'Satya' (non-violence and truth) changed the complete outlook of the Indian freedom fighters.

Mohan Das Karamchand Gandhi, also known as Mahatma Gandhi, was born on 2nd October 1869 in a Hindu family of Porbandar, Gujarat. His parents were Karamchand Gandhi and Putlibai.

His father, Karamchand Gandhi was a Diwan (Chief Minister) of Porbandar and an honourable and upright man. Gandhiji's mother was a religious and pious woman. Gandhiji gained high moral and social values from his parents. Since childhood, Gandhiji believed strongly in non-violence, truth, purity and very simple lifestyle.

At the age of 13, Gandhiji got married to a girl of the same age named, Kasturba Gandhi. They had four sons. Gandhiji started his education in Porbandar. He further studied in Rajkot and did his matriculation. Then, he joined the University of Bombay in 1887. His family wanted him to become a barrister.

# Gandhiji in South Africa

At the age of 23, Gandhiji left his family once again and came to South Africa as a legal advisor of an Indian businessman. In South Africa, Gandhiji found that there was a strong demarcation between the Black and White communities. The Black community faced a lot of discrimination and were very badly treated. Gandhiji felt very bad about this.

Just after a week of his stay, Gandhiji experienced the humiliation because of discrimination. One day, he had to travel in a train. He had a first-class ticket with him. At the Pietermartizburg station when he entered the first-class compartment and was asked to shift to the third-class compartment. The ticket checker told him that the first-class was reserved for Whites.

On raising objection on this discrimination, Gandhiji was thrown out of the train.

In 1888, he went to London for further studies and completed his law in 1891. He returned to India. For the next two years, he practised law in India.

During this journey, he late came to know that discrimination is the common practise there. The Black community and the Indians were called 'coolies'.

After this incident, Gandhiji decided to fight against this injustice. He wrote letters to the higher officials and began a protest against the discrimination in South Africa.

For the next three years, Gandhiji continuously fought for the justice. Soon, he became a well-known activist and a leader of the Indian community.

On 22nd May 1894, Gandhiji established an organisation—Natal Indian Congress (NIC) in South Africa. This organisation looked after the rights of Indians living there. While working for NIC, Gandhiji also faced a lot of opposition from the other communities. He was also attacked several times.

Gandhiji spent twenty years in South Africa. Thereafter, in the year 1915, he returned to India.

# Gandhiji in India

Gandhiji's struggles and successes in South Africa were well known in India also. He became a 'National Hero' in the eyes of Indians. Gandhiji wanted to create the same wave of reformation in India. He travelled to all the parts of India to know the real conditions of Indians.

While his travels, Gandhiji used to wear a dhoti and wooden slippers. He renounced all the pleasures and adopted a very simple lifestyle.

He established the 'Sabarmati Ashram' in Ahmedabad, Gujarat. He lived in the ashram with his family and some of his supporters. Everyone loved and supported Gandhiji.

People started believing in his teachings of non-violence and truth. He got the title of 'Mahatma', which meant 'a great soul'.

# The Indian Freedom Movement

India was under British rule at that time. A large number of freedom fighters were fighting for the freedom of India. Gandhiji also wanted the freedom of India but he followed a different path. He began a non-violent movement called 'Satyagraha' against the British.

Satyagraha means opposition, but not in an aggressive form. Gandhiji taught people to ask for justice in a silent way. The movement created a strong wave and became a great success.

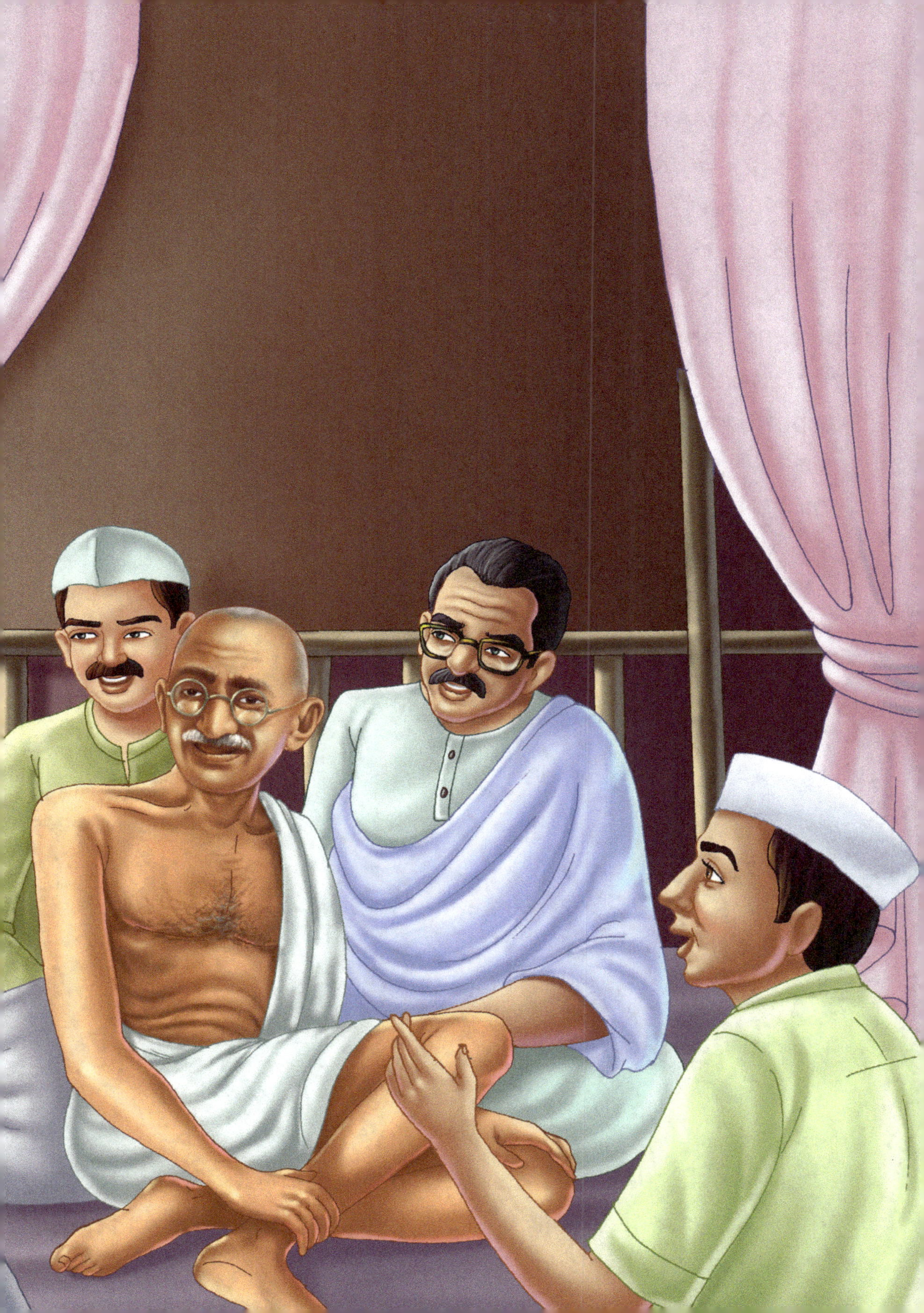

In 1919-20, Gandhiji started another movement called 'Non-cooperative movement'. During his struggle for freedom, Gandhiji was sent to jail many times by the British Govt, but he continued his mission. He asked indians to stop using foreign clothes and other things. He insisted to spin natural cloth on Charkha (spinning wheel). The image of the Charkha later became a symbol of the Indian independence.

On 12th March 1930, Gandhi ji began 'Dandi March' or the 'Salt March' against the salt tax. Gandhi ji with his supporters stand walking 200 miles from Sabarmati Ashram towards the sea.

On April 5, the group reached Dandi, a place along the Coast. Gandhiji demonstrated the method to make salt from the seawater. Soon, the movement spread in the entire nation. Gandhiji was imprisoned once again but, the protest continued nationwide. It was stopped only after the 'Delhi Pact' between the British Government and Gandhiji. The Pact granted the limited salt production and all the protestors were released.

In 1942, Gandhiji issued the last call for independence from British rule. He initiated another movement called 'August Kranti.' Soon after, he began 'Quit India' movement that asked the Britishers to leave India.

After the long struggle and sacrifices, India became independent on 15th August 1947. At the time of freedom, India faced the partition in two parts. After the freedom, Gandhiji tried to maintain peace and unity among the people of different communities.

There was a lot of disturbance in all the parts of country. The communal violence was spreading fast. To stop this violence, Gandhiji began a 'fast unto death' on 13th January 1948 which proved to be a success. On 18th January 1948, he ended his fast only when he got the assurance that the communal violence would be stopped.

# Assassination of Gandhiji

Some Indians believed that Gandhiji was responsible for the partition of India. Gandhiji faced a lot of opposition.

On the unfortunate day of 30th January 1948, Gandhiji was going to address a prayer meeting. He was walking along with his two assistants—Abha and Manu. Just when he was stepping towards the stage to address the public, a man named Nathuram Godse fired at Gandhiji.

Gandhiji fell on the ground, saying, "Hey Ram, Hey Ram!" These were the last words of Mahatma Gandhi.

The great soul, the light of the nation, was gone. The whole country was mourning bitterly on their dear Bapu's departure from the world. The other countries were also shocked at his death.

Soon after the assassination of Mahatma Gandhi, Pt. Jawahar Lal Nehru addressed the nation on radio:
"Friends & Comarades, The light has gone out of our lives and there is darkness everywhere. I do not know what to tell you and how to say it. Our beloved leader, Bapu as we called him, the Father of the Nation, is no more.
Perhaps I am wrong to say that. Nevertheless, we will never see him again as we have seen him for these many years. We will not run to him for advice and seek solace from him, and that is a terrible blow, not only to me, but also to millions and millions in this country.
And it is a little difficult to soften the blow by any other advice that I or anyone else can give you.."

# India Remembers Mahatma Gandhi

Mahatma Gandhi's Samadhi is at Raj Ghat in Delhi. Thousands of people from all over the country come to Raj Ghat to pay homage to the great man.

2nd October, Gandhiji's birthday is celebrated as 'Gandhi Jayanti'. It is one of the three National festivals of India. People of India still remember their dear 'Bapu' with great love and reverence.

Every year, 30th January—the day of Gandhiji's assassination, is observed as the Martyr's Day to commemorate the struggle of all those who sacrificed their life for the country. Mahatma Gandhi's picture is also printed on the Indian currency notes.

Mahatma Gandhi was a great writer also. He wrote and edited many newspaper articles during his lifetime. He also wrote several books including his autobiography—My Experiments with Truth.

In the year 1930, Time magazine named Mahatma Gandhi as 'The Man of the Year'. There are many books written about him and his teachings. The life of Mahatma Gandhi has been widely portrayed in the Indian literature, theatre and movies.

Mahatma Gandhi dedicated his entire life for the welfare of Indians. He has been the greatest source of inspiration for all the Indians. His teachings of non-violence, peace and truth are still practised and followed by many, not only in India but also in other countries.

The only way to pay tribute to the great man—The Father of Our Nation—is to follow his teachings in our lives. We should learn from the great life of Mahatma Gandhi.

# Chatrapati Shivaji Maharaj
# —The Great Indian Warrior

Chatrapati Shivaji Maharaj was a legendary warrior of India. He was a Maratha aristocrat of 'Bhosle' clan who founded the Maratha Empire.

Chatrapati Shivaji also founded an independent Hindu kingdom, 'Hindavi Swarajya'. He inspired and united the common man to fight against the tyranny of Mughal ruler, Aurangjeb.

Chatrapati Shivaji had extraordinary military skills. His original name was Shivaji Bhosle. He was given the title of 'Chatrapati' (sovereign) by his people, for his great capability to protect them. He has been a source of inspiration for all the generations.

# Birth and Early Years of Shivaji's Life

Shivaji was born on 19th February 1630, in the hill-fort of Shivneri in the Junnar city of Maharashtra. His father Shahji Bhosle was the leader of a band of mercenaries who served the Deccan Sultanates. His mother was Jijabai, the daughter of Lakhujirao Jadhav of Sindkhed.

Before Shivaji's birth, his mother Jijabai prayed to the local deity 'Shiva Bai' to bless her child with great skills. Shivaji was named after the deity.

Shivaji shared a very special bond with his mother. He was extremely devoted to her. She was a religious woman. Being in a religious environment with his mother, Shivaji also became highly religious. He read two great Hindu scriptures— the Ramayana and the Mahabharata.

रामायण

These two scriptures made a strong impression on Shivaji's young mind. Since childhood, he was highly inclined towards Hinduism and its dignity.
During the time of Shivaji's birth, Deccan was ruled by three Islamic sultanates—Bijapur, Ahmednagar and Golkunda. Shivaji's father lived mainly in Banglore but he

kept Jijabai and Shivaji in Poona. Jijabai's father deputed a master named Gomaji Naik Pansambal to take care of her and Shivaji.

Gomaji Naik remained with Shivaji throughout his life and played a very important role in his life. He helped Shivaji to become very strong. He gave him the training in horse riding, war skills and use of weapons. He also taught swordsmanship to Shivaji.

When Shivaji was 12-year old, he was taken to Banglore, where he received the formal training. At the age of 14, he returned to Poona with rajmudra (sovereign seal) and the council of ministers.

Shivaji was also trained by some Maratha warriors like Baji Pasalkar. He became a skilled warrior, horseman and strategist at a very young age.

Shivaji made a team of his trusted comrades and soldiers, who were mainly from the Maval region. With his team, Shivaji wandered in the hills and forests of Sahyadri region to collect information about the land.

In 1639, Shivaji led a large army of comrades, soldiers and officers.

At the age of 17, Shivaji decided to fight the sultanates. He, along with his friends, took a formal oath to free the country from the clutches of Muslim tyranny. This oath taking ceremony took place in a Lord Shiva temple in Rajreshwar. Shivaji was inspired and supported by his mother Jijabai for taking this oath.

# Confrontations and Battles of Shivaji

In the year 1645, at the young age of 16, Shivaji was ready to fight his first battle against the Sultanate of Bijapur. His first military action was attacking and capturing of the Torna Fort, which was under Bijapur sultanate.

In 1647, Shivaji attacked and captured Kondana and Raigad forts. He also got the control of most of the southern region of Poona.

In 1654, Shivaji captured the forts of Western Ghats and also the Konkan coast. In 1648-49, Adilshah imprisoned Shivaji's father. He sent an army to fight with Shivaji. Adilshah also sent an army to fight against Shivaji's brother Sambhaji at Banglore.

Both the armies of Adilshah were defeated by the Bhosle brothers. Shivaji then gained the confidence of the Mughals, who forced Adilshah to release Shivaji's father.

Adilshah then sent Afzal Khan, an experienced general to defeat Shivaji. Afzal Khan destroyed Hindu temples at Tuliapur and Pandharpur. Shivaji decided to meet Afzal Khan for negotiations. The two met at the foothills of Pratapgarh fort on 10th November 1659.

It is said that during this time, Shivaji had a vision of Goddess Bhavani. She showered her blessings on him and promised Shivaji's victory.

Before going for the meeting, Shivaji hid some weapons under his clothing and wore an armour. As custom, they embraced each other but Afzal Khan stabbed Shivaji in his back.

Shivaji's armour protected him and he survived the attack. Shivaji then counter attacked Afzal Khan with his weapons. Afzal Khan stumbled on his knees. Collapsing into a palanquin, Afzal Khan fell down. He was slain before he could do anything.

Two of the Afzal Khan's attendants attacked Shivaji. But Shivaji and Jiva Mahal (Shivaji's bodyguard) defeated them also.

After slaying Afzal Khan, Shivaji moved towards the Pratapgarh fort with his army. Shivaji's army attacked Afzal Khan's forces.

In 1666, Aurangzeb invited Shivaji and his elder son to Agra and then he imprisoned them. Shivaji made a brilliant plan to escape. He feigned a fatal sickness in the prison. He got the permission to send shipments of offerings to priests, fakirs etc., to pray for his recovery.

One day, Shivaji and his son dressed like saints hid themselves in the boxes that were to be sent as offerings. In this way, they escaped from the prison of Agra.

The most important battles and clashes of Shivaji's life were: Battle of Pratapgarh, Fall of Bijapur Army, Battle of Kolhapur, Seige of Panhala, Battle of Vishalgarh, Clash with Mughals, Battle of Umberkhind, Fight with Shaista Khan, Clash with Aurangzeb at Agra, Battle of Nesari, etc.

# Shivaji's Coronation and Rule

In June 1674, Shivaji was coronated as the king of Marathas. Under his mighty rule, the small independent land, 'Hindavi Swarajya' became a large kingdom. Hindavi Swarajya ranged from the Northwest India to the East.

Shivaji's coronation ceremony was organised in a grand manner in the Raigad fort. Thousands of people attended the ceremony. Many priests from all over came to conduct the rituals and crown the Maratha king—Chatrapati Shivaji.

After a few days of Shivaji's coronation, his mother Jijabai passed away. It was the most depressing period for Shivaji, as he was highly attached to his mother.

After sitting on the throne, Shivaji attacked and captured many places in South, like Khandesh, Phonda, Karwar, Kolhapur, Athni, Belgaum, etc.

Shivaji was a mighty ruler. His administration was also admirable. He established an able government and introduced the concepts like cabinet, foreign affairs and internal intelligence.

Shivaji had strong military powers. His military skills are compared to that of Napoleon. He used the advanced guerilla warfare tactics and intelligent networks during his battles. Shivaji also established a navy.

Shivaji had a strong bond with his people. He welcomed the people of all the sections of society to his court. He brought revolutionary changes in the welfare of the society.

By the end of Shivaji's life, he had the control of about 360 forts. He also built some new forts like Sindhudurg fort.

Shivaji was well versed in Sanskrit and Marathi languages. He had many great Sanskrit scholars and poets in his court. He promoted the use and development of Sanskrit language to a great extent.

Shivaji tried to eradicate many social issues of that time. He ended slavery in his kingdom. He also worked for the welfare and rights of women. He was successful in improving the status of women in the society.

Shivaji had eight queens. He had two sons and six daughters.

# Last Years of Shivaji's Life

In the last years of Shivaji's life, his health deteriorated drastically. After a prolonged sickness, the great Maratha king breathed his last in April 1680.

After his death, his eldest son Sambhaji sat on his throne. Shivaji is remembered and revered for his struggle against imperial powers. He became an Indian icon. Many Indian warriors and freedom fighters were inspired by his bravery and courage.

Many significant public buildings were renamed on Shivaji's name. The most important of these are Mumbai's Chatrapati Shivaji International Airport and Chatrapati Shivaji Terminus.

Shivaji has been a source of inspiration for many authors, writers, artists, poets and film directors. There are many books written on the life of Shivaji. Some movies and TV serials are also made on his heroic life.

Swami Vivekananda once said, "Shivaji is one of the greatest national saviours who emancipated our society and our Dharma when they were faced with the threat of total destruction. He was a peerless hero, a pious and God-fearing king and verily a manifestation of all the virtues of a born leader of men described in our ancient scriptures. He also embodied the deathless spirit of our land and stood as the light of hope for our future."

Shivaji's birthday, 19th February, is celebrated as 'Shivaji Jayanti' in India.

Chatrapati Shivaji taught Indians to fight for their rights and face the difficult situations with courage. We can learn a lot from Shivaji's life. His unique qualities should be inculcated to lead successful and memorable lives.

Chatrapati Shivaji Maharaj will always be remembered as a great hero of Indian history.